CONFESSIONS OF A STAR CITIZEN

Read Write Elevate

By Titanium Tem

Dedication

For My Uncle

Roderick Jerome King

Acknowledgements

I would like to thank my family and everyone who has been a friend and caring supporter of me, my dreams, and my goals. The world needs more people like you.

Contents

My Incentive to You

The focus of life is clear

Why do we lose ourselves in this time so severe?

Without fear, we must channel our inner strength and persevere because even though it may feel like the end, the beginning is so near

No matter how out of control and cold life may become, it must always be dirigible enough to steer into the right direction

Good habits eliminate neglection in any category or section of the production and progression of your life's priorities

Whether it's from following your dreams or building your self-esteem, your light is radiant and brighter than any ultra-light beam

It's the gleam in your eyes that helps you pulverize insidious negativity that transforms a captivating storm of demise into a glamorous sunrise

By no surprise are you the example of what it looks like to defeat plight, smite spite with an agape light, reverse the height of fright and disburse the bite of blight on your colorful holy and heavenly might

Your belief in a beautiful world that you perceive is what it means to live and not die

How else could you have invisible wings? They didn't teach you that you could fly

It's your imagination that keeps you determined to try

It's your spirit that keeps you echoing the aura of the mahogany reflection of the sky

This is a dominant and prominent power; use it, don't be shy

Why come down when life is meant to be lived on high?

Live your truth, for it would be a disgrace to die on a lie

Your essence is definitive way beyond barbaric or savage, so it can never be primitive

Giving you expansive faith that's extensive

Oh, and I forgot to mention with love and care for you this is my incentive

I Prefer the Former

Don't hold yourself back

Keep your mind on track and counteract slack with initiative

The objective is to not have your life be small and worthless like diminutive

Let your goals and dreams be a speculative of the life you yearn to discern and burn with a passion so fiery that your fears are placed in an urn

It's your time and turn, so aim to be number one

You'll rise high like the sun if you choose to

If you can dream of a heaven in your mind, then you can transcend out of any slum

Become numb to envious people

They're small minded, insignificant, and feeble

Getting your deserved treasure back is your ultimate retrieval

But don't lose your mind in the process

Have self-control over your gold

It'll tarnish if you stress, unless you invest in a spiritual tonic that will caress the parameters of your mind

Life is like a scavenger hunt, and we're sent here to find guidance that equals sight so we can graduate from being blind to exterminate the expansion of our perilous plight

Whether I'm wrong or right, either you're going to take flight or fight for what you believe is right

Rise Quote

We are not a basic people, so we shouldn't accept a basic lifestyle. That's totally against the coding of our DNA. When we allow ourselves to be free, no one can chain us.

I Will Rise

I will rise

I will rise to the sky

I will rise

I will rise so high

I will rise

I will rise to fly

I will rise

I will rise to your surprise

I will rise

I will rise when I try

I will rise

I will rise at an enormous size

I will rise

I will rise from being chastised

I will rise

I will rise from melancholy cries

I will rise

I will rise to be Loud

I will rise

I will rise to Stand Out in a Crowd

I will rise

I will rise knowing that I am Black and I'm Proud

I will rise

I will rise when my soul is found

I will rise

I will rise when I no longer take a seat

I will rise

I will rise when fatigue I will beat

I will rise

I will rise to be strong and not weak

I will rise

I will rise for Revolution I seek

I will rise

I will rise to be the opposite of bleak

I will rise

I will rise and be a Leader

I will rise

I will rise on Fire, the microphone Heater

I will rise

I will rise to each one, reach one, and teach one

I will rise

I will rise to Sparkle in the Sunshine

I will rise

I will rise from every metaphor or simile I write on a line

I will rise

I will rise to have Love that is so Fine

I will rise

I will rise to fly away from sin

I will rise

I will rise because I have Black Skin

I will rise

I will rise because I was born to Win

We will all Rise when we put our Minds to our Lives

And we will be High Lives instead of Low Lives

Light Quote

Remain out of sight, but if you have to be seen, make sure they see your light.

Shine

What's the object of life?

To live

What's the object of grace?

To give

See yourself for who you are because you are a bright star

You are destined to go far as your Mind travels

Unpause and solve the puzzle of life that your journey unravels

Never babble

Less words mean more, so only dabble

Be brave as you manifest what you believe in

Reality you crave, so dreams you're achieving

Never steal

Don't resort to thieving, because who can really trust a man of treason?

It's always the season to find a reason to elevate your mind to what you're perceiving

If life was a quilt, then get to weaving all the lessons and wisdom that you're receiving

Grow from your mistakes

If success was a cake, just chill and watch it bake

Understanding who you are means you are awake

What's your fate? Don't hate, turn love into something great

Steer clear of fear or else you'll be turned into shark bait

At an alarming rate, honesty always earthquakes and shakes the land of lies

Surprise! Being fake will bring your demise

So always be yourself

Expressing your soul keeps you in tip-top health

It doesn't matter if people look at you weird or what they think

What matters is that your self-esteem never ever shrinks

Your Spirit is magic, so don't jinx who you are

Because by far you're scarred as an immaculate star

You're gonna have to spar, but don't lose your self-respect

Become the architect of your life, don't neglect how you truly feel

Because that's what sets your soul free

I was determined to eternally be the greatest MC to ever be

But now I see that just doesn't sit right with me

I need to be more

Follow your spirit as your guide, and when you ride, you will soar

When you be yourself, it's always a constant war

But when you free your mind, you'll find in the game of life you'll have the highest score

Come back to the shore

The real world is the world inside and that's the one we need to explore

You'll be surprised how much power and magic you have in store

Well, all you need to do is just open the door

And SHINE, SHINE, SHINE!

IGNDTY Quote

It gets no deeper than you.

God Status (Ascending through Eternal Devotion)

In this potion I mix up a spell for devotion

A concoction that sends my mind and ideas in motion

I reach down into my subconscious mind as deep as the ocean and find ancient recipes of freedom and power created by people who look like me

With these primal eyes as my sight collectively for the future

I use them to clearly see the pre-written pages of my life

I fly with wings and cheerfully sing without stress or strife

I use these ancient eyes and I look again and I see that every lesson comprised of failure or success is a win

I look again

I see my life is prosperous beyond this earth

I stop and I think, then how high would that truly make my worth?

With these primal eyes I also have post vision

And I see that higher levels of thought represent higher levels
of living
Transcending to a new plane of reality I realize the earth is
the past
Life there was just a fad

Heart Quote

If you follow the rules, you're a fool; if you follow your heart, you rule.

The Path Is through Your Heart

Life as a writer makes me a fighter

I pick up my pen and let the ink go for a spin

Before I fail, I seek to win, which means I already won

Never jump the gun or your life will be left stunned

Paralyzed by poorly planned missions

That'll terrorize your mental and damage your psyche disposition

And leave you stranded trying to get on the bus

Spike Lee told you but the signs you didn't read, so how could you take heed?

Conduct your plans properly

One mistake could leave your passion gang raped and cost you your life

Sear through those clouded ideas with a sharp knife

And use your mind to unlock the kundalini[1] in your spine and make it right

We only get one life, so we only have one real chance to perfect the rhythm of action

And for you, I've been saving this last dance

Progress is the friend of success

Before you hate on how the next man got blessed, before you know it, look up you got next

There's no need to get upset and flex

Now it's your turn to steal the show and show the world how the magnanimous power of how your spirit can flow

Open your mind and open your eyes

And you will realize the only real lies are the thoughts you create to jeopardize your rise into gifted ascended dimensions beyond the skies

That's your only true demise

So I surmise to create a heavenly mind frame that flies

That shows the world how to truly rise

Eternal inflation is the size I expect

What could be less greater?

Be loyal not a traitor

A hater can never rise to the top floor of this infinite elevator

So make a note to self that in order for me to truly flourish into wealth, my mind and my heart have to breathe good health

Be productive and proceed

Never back track like a hairline that recedes

Follow your spirit, that's the only creed

Be your own guide, meaning be your own lead into the promised land that YOU believe

With that in mind, prosperity, confidence, and warrior stripes you will receive

But in order for this to happen, return to the source which is at the front porch of your heart

That will magnify everything you need to retrieve

[1] Kundalini(koon–duh–lee–nee)- A term deriving from Ancient India which describes a energy that is coiled at the base of your spine and that rises the higher your consciousness increases. I.E. Kundalini Rising

Grow Quote

Enhance your mentality to absorb higher vibrations so you can grow.

Grow Beyond Life

Don't limit your mind

That means don't suppress what is divine

Let your mind expand and extend

Be so real that it would be blasphemy to pretend

I grew, I evolved, and I elevated thee end

Simple as that

Life makes it complicated

Wait, question the fact

Or is complication necessary for elevation?

That's something I meditated, I started to analyze

Well that actually makes sense

In order for me to rise, there's gonna have to be turbulence

I can hear the sirens calling

And the ambulance hauling off dead body after dead body of people who couldn't manage the damage of life's frequent turbulent friction

Oh, it's real like nonfiction

It's a truth of living that's not a fairytale

In order to excel you must balance good and malice on a spiritual scale

Grow within and find your inner Zen to prevail

This is what separates the hard and the strong from the weak and the frail

From the day you're born, you're indulged in an inner war

Your passion should be shaped and centered like the earth's core

Material things and smiling faces can be an illusion to trap you in the allure of not seeing someone's true intensions which could actually involve gore

Listen to your spirit

It'll tell you the answers and ethics you need to stampede hate, envy, jealousy, and greed to breed a mind of spectacular, vernacular, Excalibur power that was freed from you following your inner guidance as a lead into a promised land no man can reprimand but you only if you believe

So hear it

We have the power to move mountains and Giza pyramid-sized pillars

And drink at the fountains of self-love which is the most potent elixir

Become a self-healer

It is our birthright to ignite the pulsars of light that make us shine so bright we eliminate spite

Construct your vision to be clear

With clarity you can spread your dreams across the entire world hemisphere

Save your own life first, that's sincere

And then you'll be revered as a hero and cherished as a sacred symbol and become a world example of how to destroy fear

The Real Shore

Words of wisdom lie in the depths of love

Fly in a space above your own comprehension

Sharing knowledge is allowing your mind to be an extension
of elevated intension

Actions scream louder than words

So I'm going to perform the right acts to help me share the
sky with the birds

My wings are intact as I gear to take flight

Fear holds you back and clouds your third eye's sight

So how can you soar if your mind's eye is sore?

Swap earth for heaven to make a divine floor of mystical lore
that creates an encyclopedia of spells to help you evaporate
self-destruction from your pores and excel on an envisioned
trail of success that abhors hell and that tests your mind to
invest in doubting yourself less for you to prevail

Open the door, because when you do, you'll see there's light
at the core

Be the water of your higher conscious and flow back to the genius in yourself

That's the Real Shore

Real Wealth Pt.1

You are the key

In order to unlock sight, you must have the right eyes to see

The only person that you should be searching to be is you

Always remain true or your spirit will catch the flu

Which is something no pharmaceutical over-the-counter medicine can cure

That's a spiritual sickness which needs a healing that is pure

The best option is to understand how much falsehood you can endure

And understand when it's time to fly away from lies

You have to be sure

The less you stress, the easier the test

In order to do your best, you must confess within

How true to yourself are you?

Would you neglect yourself or strive to correct yourself?

Would you invest in the overall productivity of your health or befoul your gold and tarnish your wealth?

Whether you level up or down, you wear the crown. because no matter what, only you can free yourself to expand and make your life profound

For Original People Like You

My People

My People

Have we forgot

Or have we just didn't know?

That when it comes to our Black History our minds pick up slow

Yeah when it comes to your History you shrug your shoulders or roll your eyes

But it was our leaders who fought for our freedom instead of demise

I can see that it's plain to see that you don't care

But tell me what ancestors are in the roots of your hair?

How come Black is the race to attack?

I thought we were Brothers and Sisters or is it too much crack?

Must we close our eyes to the truth at hand?

Or must we open our eyes to another wine bottle or beer can?

It isn't safe to say that we have reached our goal

But as far as being BLACK, have we met our role?

They call us Nigga, monkey, or junkie

But can you ask yourself, "Has America really struck me?"

Are you surprised nowadays when you see a Black Revolutionist?

Or are you convinced that our so-called freedom lives don't need any more Activists?

Being born Black, it's a struggle but it has a special gift

Be honest with yourself, when it comes to learning your history, do you plead the fifth?

I'm not talking about world history or American history because you were forced to learn that in school

But learning your Black History, does it really matter if you're cool?

We fought for no segregation

We fought for integration

But has integration caused us to lose sight on our own information?

My People

My People

I am told that back in the day we had so much finesse

But when I look into today, we are not the same

Do you have shame from where you've came?

Or is this country the residence you claim?

We've come so far from wearing a conk

But in February, do you learn and learn in Black History Month?

After the 28th. do you ignore and snore yourself to sleep, no longer expanding your mind with your History?

Forgetting who we really are and where we really came from is our biggest crime, our mystery

So here I am again asking you an important question

My People

My People

Do we really know ourselves or are we brainwashed from American TV?

Or is there confusion plain to see or is there hidden confusion that is not to be seen?

My People

For years we have been terrorized, traumatized, and stigmatized

A part of why is because we did not have the Power and the Knowledge to Fight back

Don't you realize knowing our History is our true freedom?

Our Ancestors went through Hell more than once for us. Will you ever redeem them?

Being Black you are owed a large debt

Read your History

Because you owe a large debt to Yourself

Operation Save Black Gold

Black people need to be free

We need to open our mind's eye so we can clearly see

Emphatically we have to strategically fight

We graphically have to take this stance as soon as tonight

At an oxygen height we need to be able to breathe and inhale

how high we can excel

We must prevail against any calamity that will knock us off of

our trail unless our passion will be left pale, cold, and frail

And so when we try to eat the fruits of our labor for it not to

taste stale

Black people we are in hell and our mind is the cell

So don't let them trick you in a mental prison free yourself

on your own bail

That's real

Love is something you can feel

Well we should fly like doves and produce energy to heal

Become inspiration for the whole black nation to rise to a higher station

That's a beautiful elation that's never on probation

The path of harmonious wraith is within us

Like when guns bust let's bang with trust

Let's impact our growth through organized combat and use hope when there's nothing left to get us back on track

But we need definite answers of our future

When our minds are refined we transform and become aligned as a united shooter against foes that are pros at giving us woes but truthfully we must be on our P's and Q's and on the tips of our toes to detonate the blues of a black self-destructive muse so our light and ultimate strike can glisten and glow as true freedom

Our life struggle is the answer to these clues

Let's be our own world news

This world is ours literally

To keep it we have to channel and enhance our powers mystically

The imagination can blow like rocket ship thrusters explode so ignite your inner might like a bomb and implode

Let this be the start of the meditation for the elevation code of the people of Gold

Become Quote

I just want to become who I already am.

Bring out my power from within and shine my light in all directions.

Become New

Emancipate your soul and stand firm against the world

Don't forget your light has value; you're gifted like gold, diamonds, and pearls, so hurl all you have and give it your best shot because the victory of this is only meant for you; this is your ordained slot

Break those chains, keep your Black slang, and use your brain to rise to the top

Black success will never flop if you treat it as private stock that you can invest in to win

They prey on your life to end, so put a spin on the future and show them that you can ascend

Dedication is the fuel behind the dollars I spend, so make Black freedom be a permanent style instead of a trend to blend with other anecdotes of internal salvation

Cut the noose rope and hang the American nation for persecuting Black skin for shining like a shen ring and for our spirits sparkling brighter than jewelry exemplifying ultimate bling, bling

The task is at hand

The reflection of our minds should be the reflection of the land we occupied before invasion gentrified us out of our Egyptian sands

Blowing off our divine snouts making us unidentifiable even to our own selves

Mind wiping

That's God identity sniping

Even a Pharaonic brown-black face looks peculiar yet still unfamiliar even when we're skyping

Ultra-invincible DNA is the message I'm typing in the blueprint of my subconscious mind that's the representation of backbone and a crystalized spine

Gold pumping through our veins that's royal blood

Angelic floods of my young black generation transforming into the personification of liberation

This is our soul journey destination

Living life free as our occupation

Shape shifting reality by destroying gravity so we can levitate upwards in hordes toward our greatness

Through self-love we lead a life that stampedes self-hate

A victorious breed of Black people that can never break

We stand as divine gems

Our souls sing freedom hymns while running through the underground railroad of sweet dreams and a distinctive hope that one day they come true

Sticking together, clutching each other like glue, we are the answer to the tale of the caged bird that flew

Transforming our lives and redesigning the murals of our minds, conveying powerful images of us portraying a magical imagination, giving us wings that we can use to fly in real life

The time has come for us to not be dumb but to be smart and follow our heart and be numb to nefarious spirits that desire to tear us apart

Neutralize that scum with your Black magic, Black excellence; your Black mind is your natural intelligence and realizing that gives you a head start

Every war won is mental, so in order to keep score, keep track of how aggressive you attack and where you need to be gentle

The system of elevation lives inside of you

Reawaken what was once taken that is now retrieved and blossom and believe that you can unlock your hidden powers and become anew

Sun Energy (Sunergy) meaning

The brightest light to give to a planet transcribing from your spirit.

Invincible Light (Sun Energy)

I am great beyond light years to come, so how could I be and act so dumb?

Can't I see that I am the way, the truth, and the path to enlightenment?

Not trying to spark my inner flame, abandoning it and leaving it dark is a betrayal to my own consignment

My inner dreams are pertinent

Leaving them behind, I ask myself is it worth it?

It can't be, because I wouldn't feel them floating inside my spirit for nothing

Living my truth and being 20/20 living proof of my dreams being accomplished means I can never be bluffing

So then that's the dedication

For my life to kiss the lips of elevation, it's going to take the emancipation of my inner shackles that I placed on myself to explode and crackle so I can narrate my internal exoneration story of how I bloomed into the mahogany abyss of liberation

That involves no castration but a benevolent meditation of pulchritudinous clear blue skies set aside for my magnificent levitation, my rise

Achievement and a life well fulfilled is my destination

I tackle these vices that die with large prices because freedom ain't free

This Black boy would rather build pyramids that poke holes in the sky then be cuffed, stuffed, charged and booked and barged into a prison cell full of other mistreated and misguided Black males who's life trail is on a roller coaster ride faster into deeper hell by a system that laid traps for us to fail created by a prejudice people who saw us unfit to enjoy the world's beauty and rediscover the treasures our ancestors left for us to inherit to keep the power of our great golden legacy evolving for our future generations to come just because of the color and incomparable mysticism of our outer shell

That's not a fate my family would want for me

And truthfully I know that would shatter my mother's heart to pieces to know that her baby boy she carried in her precious God womb for nine months was prematurely placed in a tomb for attempting to give the world the Sun Energy he has to offer bestowing an exceptional soul of an ancient man with skin of copper that may have light that is too bright for some dark souls to intake

I wouldn't want that fate for myself

So I made a choice; I'm bookmarking every page of my life with an oath of elevation

Every day and night I'm going to shine my light so radiantly that I help those carrying souls that resemble busted bulbs from hurt and insecurity to find their electric currents and purity so they can shine like the stars they came from again

That's an ultimate win

Every day and night I'm going to treat my mind like a goldmine and offer the best elevating, empowering, and nurturing thoughts to give to my family and friends and autonomously send agape love to them and any other doves with fractured wings, helping to heal a spirit with powers that's Bombay so that maybe one day they can take air to the sky so their souls can be at peace and sing

Every day and night I promise to give myself the best self-love I possibly can so that I can send this same Rose Energy to those that need it to better love themselves immensely

I promise to program my subconscious mind with repetitive symbols of positive power to give to the planet every minute, second, and hour

For my entire being this is the man my Capstone Eye is seeing

This is an oath of elevation to myself that would obligate me to contribute the richness of the world's wealth

Why not be a better man for myself so that I can be a better man for others?

In the galactic DNA of my soul, I couldn't think of anything better

So no matter the weather, I will always present Sun Energy to the planet to make this elevation oath shine true and use and expand every corner of my mind to infuse the land beneath my feet

I stand firm on my two feet and walk forward; I'll never retreat

The path of this Black boy embodies the wraith of all the ancient and ancestral Black men that came before me

Invincible light

That's my principal sight

I'm a Titan from the stars, so it's my divine right to fight for the existence of my celestial identity using the eyes of my spirit as my sight

I'm using my will to fight for a reality I believe is tranquil

This world needs more High Energy to rebuttal suicidal misery

In this lifetime, I'm taking responsibility to give something greater than I ever have before

We've been losing for too long, so now it's time to even the score and surpass

Ah last! The people who have been deemed heavenly outcast are no longer last

This Black man, this Titan will be a helping hand to this reality manifesting in a flash

The Secret of Life Quote

Your Imagination is reality and your reality is just your Imagination. Project what you want to see and control it.

A Starseed's Self-Security

I didn't come to this world to care about you laughing at me

I came here to free me

Expressing my soul

Expressing my spirit is the whole goal

And plus taking back the mind that was stole

That's the price you pay for living on earth, a lethal toll

And every piece recovered represents a rebirth so I've been reincarnating every day

Something that's real in this fake world is what everyone is searching for

Fake, fake

I take a rake and bag up the leaves of your lies because it's bringing down my soul's property value

My motive couldn't be too true

Confessions of A Star Citizen

Write to open my mind and dump out my feelings

But on the outside in public, I'm concealing the truth I hold inside

It's delicate and very fragile

But I will live and die for it and run an infinite number of miles to see it manifest and come into fruition

I been the best that was told to me by my intuition

I signed a spirit petition that was dedicated to freeing myself out of my cell of a shell because holding yourself back is just creating invisible prison bars on your mind

So who's the real warden?

I'm boarding a flight to the stars because I'm tired of dumbing myself down to fight in earthly spars

It's energy draining

I'm using celestial fuel

Dressing to impress

Stressing and being obsessed over material decreasing value items and fake people battling over who's most cool

Emphatical fools

Finessing their phony styles and debating over who's the stool

I'd rather be backstroking in Saturn's free world pools

I adore my imagination

Not using it is like putting my dreams on probation

So who's the real parole officer?

Power has been in my possession since birth

Only earth has taught me how to decrease my worth and lower my standards when I am a higher standard

Where I'm from I used to buggy board on the milky way coastline

I didn't have to wonder whether or not I was divine

That thought wouldn't even exist in my mind

Reality became whatever I thought it to be and then it was

So who's really Supreme?

Because when I use my mind, I can transform my life to live my most magnificent dream

The fire of my faith is the ultimate stich in that celestial seam

Magic Woman

Magic Women are the greatest

The most loved and the most hated

They are the highest rated women on the earth

To the whole world they gave birth to every civilization that
exists

I persist to dismiss all notions of wannabe exotic women cause
it's a lame mix

Unfavorable people bash Magic Women in the dust and
rather not love her but only invest in her for lust and misuse
her trust

Those men truly create a universe of disgust trying to abuse
and rust out a woman's healing powers

Making her feelings toward compassionate men who really
want to love her sour

Magic Woman you are the icon at the top of my tower

I'll devour all infestations of pests that threaten the safety of
our nest where the children of our nation will sleep and rest

Magic Woman let me be your strength when you are weak every week and let's not be separate let's be together and seek in harmony, love, and peace with intertwined hearts for balanced mobility a kingdom of complicity to reap

Take my hand, the hand of a real Magic Man who wants to take a chance with you and leap

You're the only woman I would rather have, so I would die if I couldn't have my better half

Magic Woman YOU are my strength

Magic woman YOU are the RULER I use to measure the greatness of my talents' length

Without you how can I prosper?

Without communication how can our relationship foster?

I communicate this life-transforming passionate love to you

Let's Have A World-Changing Love

Magic Woman you are the black dot in the center of my eye
Contrary to how you may feel just know you're too wonderful to irritate me like a sty
Madame Supreme you are too fly
I treasure your mind as a beautiful delicacy when we can share and combine our thoughts and have sapient dinner in the living room of our aligned and intertwined transparent frequencies
That's a meal that is most divine because the more I get to know you the more I can understand the history and root of your shine and that allows me to be able to notate and rate the level and timing of how and when I can project mine
See sister, when we get to know each other with the purest intensions we create a relationship that's a win- win
Our love can never go out of style, so there's no such thing as this being a trend

I want to love you so hard that I can feel your heart beating in my chest as if I had two

Is that too crazy or can we be the example of a forgotten level of love to this world and make them think its brand new?

Double the hearts means double the blood flow which means double the power

Wherever we go this heart transplant can be seen through our eyes as the symbolic sacred love that we sow

Why have a love that's mediocre?

Why not have a love worth living, growing, and being our best for?

Remember we're above this earth anyway, so let's have solar system sex to open a portal to higher worlds so this world can see where and how it needs to improve

The melody of our chemistry can be the world's new rhythmic groove and tone for the soundtrack of serenity and tranquility spawning from our translucent remarkable love for each other revolving in continuity

Whenever we get the urge to sexually merge let's become a beacon of an empowering surge of divine companionship sent to purge all nefarious forces that seek to make this world weak and divide us from each other in an attempt to blow out the fire of our connected torches

Let's come together and change the world with our souls and become inseparable mates

And master the winds of wisdom to control our fates

Magic Woman let's elevate and have a world-changing love

The Commitment

My paper is the water and my pen is the raft that I use to cruise and pedal myself across the oceans of emotions that I endure and conjure inside because my heart is the map I choose

I don't want to run and hide

I'd rather stand like a man with pride and heal like peroxide and slide for what I feel

I am committed to myself

The dedication of the elevation of my precious wealth

My love for this in my heart couldn't be more pure

I am confident I will shine my light, I am sure

Actually I'm shining now

Like a gun goes pow!

MY MAGIC IS LIKE WOW!

A redeeming sorcerer gleaming through a mysterious corridor

What awaits on the other side is unknown

I hope it's an honorable man that's full grown

A dream of a future me that the mirror has shown

I'm magical to the bone and reflect the image of infinity

MY SOUL IS A SHRINE OF SELF-LOVE,

SELF HATE CAN NEVER CROSS MY LINE OF
SYMMESTRY

Investing In your Growth Is the Right Way

Follow your dreams and don't fold

Wisdom is the way, so follow your empirical thoughts and never stray

Don't let anyone change your mind for lesser

Your vision is the treasure and you are the grand finesser of that prolific prime paradigm

Don't be a follower be a leader

Subtracting time into yourself makes you hollower

Being honest makes you a truth seeker

How plain for your membrane can this be communicated?

Your hidden greatness is like finding a lost Egyptian pharaoh to be excavated

Don't be eliminated from the trail of your inner self-discovery or else you'll be rushed into mental cardiac recovery

Repetitively losing your mind is the summary

That's clear redundancy

Invest in your growth

To sleep on your rise means you aren't woke

Don't cloak and run away when life gets too hard

Your destiny is meant for you to unlock and attain and your courage is your keycard

The gateway of greatness calls for your patience

Nothing worth having is gained overnight

So be vigilant toward your growth because eventually, if you tread fearlessly, every caterpillar transforms into a beautiful butterfly to take flight

Help Me to Fly

The task is at hand

Be united like dreadlocks in a society that's deadlocked
instead of individual strands

Take a stand for something greater than yourself

To be clear in order to be revered it's better to cherish than
perish your inner wealth

Be yourself, satisfaction is guaranteed

Indeed to make the choice to do that means you planted the
first seed

Read to elevate your mind

In time knowledge will be the first power in the final hour to
help you unleash your Sunshower

Your light is most divine

Just do your best

Never rest until you transform into a full moon from a crest

The permission from your intuition is the first sign

Activate your duty

Eradicate the lust to always chase booty

Spread information

If you know something I don't know, I welcome you to please come and school me

Don't be selfish

You never know, love may be what I need to replenish when I'm about to diminish

Blossom into Your Power

Pay attention

Making bad decisions can be the price of life and that's a detrimental pension

If you want a new life you have to use courage to kill strife

Even if your clout was too ripe, you'll still see the light

Your reflection is number one, so that's only who you obey

Stay on the path, stay focus, don't ever stray

So when the time comes you'll have enough power to slice and slay

Block stereotypes

Believing in those is like believing the hype

Treat them like a screen swipe and slide them out the way

Believing in yourself and following your own mind is having a brighter day

Be Malcolm or Che'

Or combine both energies to intertwine a cherishable power that's divine with ultimate synergy to change the future of time

Please, no misery taught in my history

We invented science, mathematics, architecture and chemistry

Everything under the sun is a part of our ministry and everything over the stars and afar is a product of our spirit body's testimony

Why be phony when you were born real?

Don't let this fabricated world steal your originality

You can rise like a sparrow while they're still trying to defy gravity

You are the majesty of your own royal kingdom of liberation

Become pure in the passion of your heart

That's your first nation

Then transport your power from there to execute actions of elevation to have a better world of creation

The realization of who you really are is your greatest manifestation

Awaken Your Ultimate Greatness

I have to spark and eat jealous punks like a shark for trying to dwindle my light dark

The swindle of life can touch the heart, though that's where you start to know how things fall apart

Struggle can stink like a fart but those that rise and come out on top are an example of who's smart

Life is just a mental exhibition match

Improve the rendition of your ascension to open the hatch and add more weapons to your batch

Make moves that are smooth but don't lose the rhythm of your groove by paying attention to others

Losing focus on yourself is like blowing your cover

Did I mention you are the serum to the disease you're sick from?

Peace of mind can be developed in seconds just from a simple hum

Stick to positive vibes like gum

And if someone doesn't budge don't judge, because not
everyone plays to the same beat as your drum
Ignoring the guidance of your spirit is dumb
You might as well be homeless inside living like a bum
Following wisdom can keep you out of prison
Stepping into your power is the same as like seeing Christ
arisen
Make the decision
How would you know what you're missing if you continue
to diss your soul and never listen?
Truth eventually unfolds no matter how long it takes
You have the power of an earthquake
Which means you're in control of what stays fixed and what
breaks

Waves of Compassion

Be strong and put weakness on the shelf

And leave it to rotten, forgotten

Move on and levitate higher because it's dire

Your spirit is infinite, so how could you retire?

The sole goal is to live beyond the Earth

Your soul is gold, which is more valuable than worth

I'm picking up clues that ensue we're divine beyond birth

Heal don't hurt

The code I implode is self-care, so give yourself a growth

spurt

It's better to share, so let comradery blow like a snare

And if you're in need of a shoulder to lay on, I have a spare

Without Love you impair

Levitate

Justice means peace

How can violence cease if you haven't tamed the beast?

That's a ten-ton question

A suggestion I advise is to use viewer discretion and organize your mind with the utmost protection so this world made of lies won't corrupt your rise or grangerize your fate

Put on your superhero cape to change the shape of your life to have better character traits to help you escape bad habits that can easily tape on-going failure behavior

Be your own savior

The lessons of life help you see the blessings of strife

You are the President, District Attorney, Governor, and Mayor of your life's purpose

If you were born, how could you ever be worthless?

That's a Divine Law

Don't let this physical world puzzle you like a jigsaw

I hope you heard this

Serenity of The Mind
(The Healing Center)

Fly

That's all I want to do and chew achievement like it's beef
stew

No sadness

Only gladness as I race to my destiny like Sonic destroying
Professor Badnic

My vices?

That's what entices the gamble dices

The temptation is high, so I fight this by writing this

Don't hiss

Only dismiss piss scent words that fall from spiteful lips

Don't trip from their words

Use your thoughts to transform into an onslaught of a school
of birds

And fly to a place of serene scenery

Maybe somewhere with endless lush greenery

A place of plush energy

Somewhere mahogany void of misery

And envision yourself as a dynamic diamond radiating with all your brilliance shining as an invincible inviolable symbol of resilience and allow your avatar like jeweled persona to glow like the infinite stars you descended from

Your home is where you have peace, so if your thinking is tranquil how can this comeliness decease?

This is a way to heal and build an inner majestic fortress of courage that causes fear to yield and that seals the escape of your untapped potential

Let this mind power be your shield in a world of unwavering calamity

It's essential

Untitled

At an old stage I was a bird caged full of rage looking to find clarity and peace through sage

If my mind was a gun, I'd blast positivity and peace vibes at everyone until they were numb

And make them drunk off love like rum

Yeah that'll be fun

Why wait for daylight when your spirit is the sun?

Bust a Hole in the Sky

The sky is not the limit

That's a consistently sold gimmick that leaves too many people's vision left cold, dry, and timid

I believe it's imperative to see vivid dreams that allow you to breathe beyond the sky

If you don't fly or question why you won't try, you have nothing left to do but die

So use your imagination to find the tools for the root work you need for conjuring a better nation from your mind

Do not involve procrastination

Because that's an entity that helps you invest in losing time

The Anecdote Is You

If you had the chance to be great would you take it?

It seems like all my generation does is sleep and complain

Do you know how much money and opportunity there is out here to be gained?

To believe you can achieve success overnight is truly insane

Well maybe if you worked a couple of strong roots and spells

But if you want to excel, you're going to have to walk a less favorable trail

You should let your mind set sail on the voyage of unfiltered elevation

To give a notable success story should be your ultimate dedication and to have a legacy to leave behind

The clues have always been evident; you just have to read the signs and you will understand that the divine is at your mental crafting table when you reshape and refine your life

Wait, let me back up, not all of my generation is poor and lazy

The other half is deeply bathing in success so much you would think I'm crazy

The key ingredient to success is to harness that with which you have been blessed and master that skill or talent like you've been obsessed

You are the way, the light, and the truth, so if you reversed the belief of that on yourself as far as greatness is concerned, you would be living proof

How long will you gaze at the stars before you shoot for them?

Remember you were born with light

Don't let this world turn down the dial of your shine and make you dark and dim

This message is straight from my heart aimed at yours, sincerely Titanium Tem

Made in the USA
Columbia, SC
12 December 2022

72579725R00046